IMAGES OF
MERSEYSIDE

Liverpool ECHO

IMAGES OF
MERSEYSIDE

Breedon Books
Publishing Company
Derby

First published in Great Britain by
The Breedon Books Publishing Company Limited
Breedon House, 44 Friar Gate, Derby, DE1 1DA.
1994.

Softback edition 1998

ISBN 1 85983 114 1

Printed and bound by Butler & Tanner Ltd., Selwood Printing Works, Caxton
Road, Frome, Somerset.

Covers printed by Lawrence-Allen, Weston-super-Mare, Avon.

Contents

Introduction

ALTHOUGH traditionally a part of Lancashire, Liverpool, the huge focal point of Merseyside, has an atmosphere and a character quite unlike the rest of the county.

Virtually close to communities still retaining the general county accent, it has developed a 'voice' all of its own. This undoubtedly originates from its main, mixed population of Lancastrians, Irish, Welsh and Scots.

The world knows this accent as 'Scouse' and Liverpudlians as 'Scousers'.

The accent has spilled over into surrounding areas, like Birkenhead and Wirral and, with so many Merseysiders having been engaged world-wide in maritime and military operations and so on, it is small wonder that 'Scouse' (originally an old name for a type of stew) is now usually associated with the people of Liverpool.

Liverpudlians' general friendliness, hospitality and good humour is renowned and tremendous goodwill and affection for the city and its people have accrued.

Liverpool has grown from a small fishing village, which incorporated a creek off the tidal River Mersey. Not surprisingly, even the Romans moving thereabouts bypassed it and missed its maritime potential.

In August 1207, King John granted Liverpool a Charter, and from a borough it progressed steadily towards the important city and port that it became.

The town once had a 13th-century castle, dominating a promontory where creek and river met - the area now called Derby Square. The castle saw very little warlike action and was demolished early in the 18th century.

One who especially noted Liverpool's rapid growth was Daniel Defoe (author of *The Life and Adventures of Robinson Crusoe*) who, on his third visit and finding the town considerably larger, increasing in wealth, business and buildings, declared: "What it may grow to in time, I know not." Defoe would have been amazed had he lived to see the later incredible progress of Liverpool, when it boasted the enviable title of 'Second City of the Empire.'

The following years witnessed vast expansion of trade, building and population, embracing the whole of Merseyside. In the last century, Liverpool's great granite docks spread northwards to Bootle, near the estuary, making seven miles in all by early this century. Docks were also built on the Wirral side of the Mersey, at Birkenhead and Wallasey, as the region's vast maritime business grew. Ships from every maritime nation called here.

Merseyside's golden chapter in sea-going history reveals the world's greatest names in shipping being closely associated with Liverpool, the nearest deep-sea port in Europe to America. In fact, Liverpool is the major UK port for trade with the eastern seaboard of North America.

Famous lines included Allan, Alfred Holt, Bibby, Brocklebank, Black Ball, Booth, Canadian Pacific, Collins, Cunard, Donaldson, Elder Dempster, Furness Withy, Guion, Inman, Lamport and Holt, Leyland, Pacific Steam Navigation, Warren and White Star.

The Liverpool liners were also known worldwide. So many of them sailed from the Mersey over some 130 years. A few even acquired almost-legendary status - like the first *Mauretania* (sister of the ill-fated *Lusitania*), which held the Blue Riband of the Atlantic for 22 years.

During the last world war, Liverpool became the most important port in Europe, so vital to the Allied cause, and masses of war material from America poured in.

Here, too, was the top-secret 'nerve-centre' for the Battle of the Atlantic, controlling convoys and escorts and general anti-U-boat operations. This interesting, historic headquarters, located below Derby House, has been fully restored and is now known as Western Approaches and open to the public.

Although the liners have now gone, trade in the Port of Liverpool is still brisk and flourishing. The huge, modern Royal Seaforth Docks' complex, and the highly successful 640-acre Freeport, record steadily increasing traffic and business.

Great wealth was amassed in Victorian Liverpool from big business in shipping, commerce and banking. Those were the days when King Cotton ruled in Lancashire, too. Merseyside's numerous large warehouses were filled with a wide variety of imports from all over the world.

Sadly, this prosperity, which afforded so many grand homes and estates in the suburbs of the city and across the river, did little to improve the lot of the majority of citizens, who worked long and hard hours for relatively little pay, and thousands of poor folk relied on charity.

Still, Liverpool deservedly boasts a proud record of culture and higher learning. Some fine institutions, including the Literary and Philosophical Society and the Royal Institution, were created here in the late 18th and early 19th centuries. Today, the city possesses two universities in the University of Liverpool, (founded as a college in 1882 and established by Charter in 1903) and the new John Moores University, established in 1992.

The city has led the country, and even the world, in 'firsts' in so many fields. A major example is that the first real passenger and freight railway, George Stephenson's Liverpool & Manchester Railway, was opened in Liverpool in 1830.

Liverpool, of course, had its darker side. It will always be associated with the major British role it played in the loathsome slave trade, until dedicated abolitionists, including citizens like William Roscoe, William Rathbone and others, helped put an end to it.

British participation in the slave trade was made illegal on 1 May 1807, and the hard-bitten traders operated until the last day.

Over the centuries many of the seagoing fraternity from other lands have made Liverpool their home. But the greatest influx came in the 1840s when countless Irish folk arrived here after fleeing from their homeland during the terrible potato famines. Thousands of them emigrated to the New World via Liverpool and many of them, with precious few possessions and no money for transatlantic passages, stayed put in Liverpool.

Here they settled, generally in appalling living conditions and poverty.

On a brighter note, it is not surprising that, with such prevalent good humour and quick wit hereabouts, the Liverpool area has produced so many comedians, not to mention producers, playwrights and stars of stage, film and television. Look at this random, mixed bag of well-known names - a list certainly not complete:

Bill Kenwright, Willy Russell, Alan Bleasedale, Carla Lane, Beryl Bainbridge, Arthur Askey, Tommy Handley, Ken Dodd, The Beatles, Jimmy Tarbuck, Rex Harrison, Ted Ray, Dereck Guyler, Cilla Black, Frankie Vaughan, Tom O'Connor, Derek Nimmo, Leonard Rossiter, John Gregson, Alberto Remedios, Rita Hunter, Gerry Marsden, the McGann Brothers, Stan Boardman . . .

However, for the millions of visitors from home and abroad who come to Liverpool, it is not just the Beatles' haunts that they discover! They also marvel at the city's architectural wonders, which include the magnificent Anglican and Roman Catholic Cathedrals, the Queensway and Kingsway Mersey Tunnels, linking the city with the Wirral Peninsular, St George's Hall and the Town Hall, and streets of conserved Regency and Victorian buildings and residences, all of which attract so many film-makers.

Merseyside has many glorious parks and open spaces and there are long promenades on both sides of the river. Standing on Liverpool's Otterspool Promenade, overlooking Wirral (which has its own beauty spots) and the North Wales mountains, it is hard to believe that one is so close to a big city.

Merseyside also possesses two popular seaside resorts in New Brighton, at the end of the peninsular, and Southport, along the sandy, wooded coast to the north of the city. Southport, of course, has the world-famous Royal Birkdale Golf Course, a nationally-famous annual flower show, a superb boulevard and many holiday attractions.

As for football, the supporters of Everton, Liverpool and Tranmere FCs are renowned for their fervour, loyalty - and knowledge of the game!

Hundreds of acres of derelict docks and riverside have been converted into interesting centres of entertainment, shopping, business and water sports. Some of the giant 19th-century warehouses of brick and iron, now accommodate luxury flats.

The Albert Dock complex alone - incorporating the fascinating Merseyside Maritime Museum - forms the largest collection of Grade 1-listed buildings in Europe.

Former vast areas of decaying waterfront property and land were also transformed into the glorious International Garden Festival, opened by the Queen in 1984, when it became the biggest tourist magnet in Britain, attracting 3.5 million visitors. Most of this area is now occupied by a large and attractive leisure centre - 'Pleasure Island'.

In this book we look at a great variety of subjects, including Royal visits, transport, entertainers, the scars of war, and the changing face of the city and the port.

This splendid collection of pictures will evoke a host of memories of places, events and people, covering numerous aspects of Merseyside's colourful canvas.

Derek Whale
June 1994

Ancient Liverpool

The earliest known view of Liverpool (*c.*1160-1189), showing the castle with the creek, or 'Poole', rounding to the extreme right; also the ancient chapel of Our Lady, on which site the Church of St Nicholas and Our Lady now stands.

Custom House and Old Dock, built on the site of the Pool, which was impounded by floodgates to become the first commercial wet dock in England, keeping vessels afloat at all stages of the tide.

Part of the south side of Dale Street in 1850. A number of coaching inns were located in this area.

Some Liverpool Landmarks

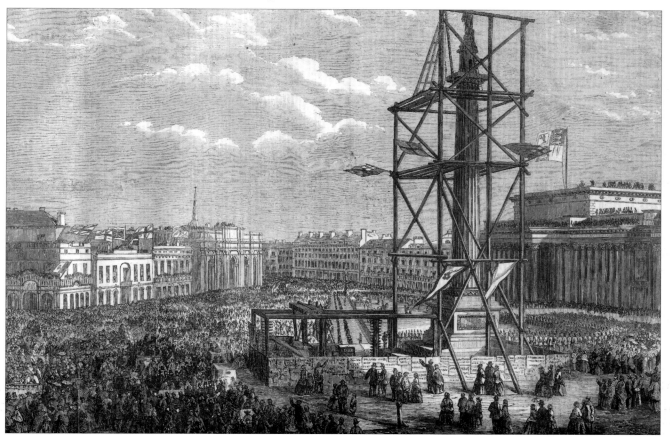

The unveiling of Liverpool's memorial to the Duke of Wellington (the 'Iron Duke'), on 16 May 1863.

The 'new' North Western Hotel, Lime Street, as it was in 1870, adjoining the station.

The massive Greco-Roman, Grade 1-listed building of St George's Hall, with Plateau and Cenotaph, dominates Lime Street.

An inspiring view of the giant Corinthian columns forming the hall's 200ft long colonnade.

This splendid Great Hall, within St George's Hall, with its superb tiled floor and huge organ, and also its Golden Concert Hall, have awed hundreds of thousands of guests and visitors for 150 years.

Liverpool Town Hall - the city's third, and a Grade 1-listed building - was built in 1749-54, although restoration followed a big fire in 1795.

The magnificent interior of the Town Hall has been praised by Royalty. This is part of the large ballroom.

Members of Liverpool City Council make municipal history for this mayor-making ceremony in the Town Hall on 15 May 1972. The Council, as then constituted, was to be the last before local government reorganisation.

This stately complex of buildings, in William Brown Street, incorporates the main Museum, Libraries and Art Gallery.

John Moores University, formerly the Liverpool Polytechnic. The complexes of both universities cover many acres of the city.

University of Liverpool's original red-brick building and clock tower. Formerly University College, it was created Liverpool University by Royal Charter in July 1903.

A background of storm clouds and sunshine creates a dramatic picture of the 450ft St John's Beacon in August 1973.

Huge, old St John's Market, a favourite city shopping centre in Elliot Street/Great Charlotte Street, was opened in 1822 and only demolished after nearly 150 years.

Modern second St John's Market, destroyed by fire in December 1977, was rebuilt and re-opened in November 1981.

A new landmark for Liverpool is the ultra-modern Queen Elizabeth II Law Courts, Derby Square, opened by the Queen in May 1984. It contains 28 courtrooms.

The *Daily Post & Echo's* old offices and printing works in Victoria Street, with van fleet awaiting editions.

Grand symbol of 1930s architecture, George's Dock Building, at Mann Island, serving as offices and a Queensway Tunnel ventilation shaft.

One of Liverpool's oldest city buildings, Bluecoat Chambers, originally built in 1717 as a charity school.

Merseyside at War –1914-18

Women take over the road-sweeping jobs of men at the front (1916).

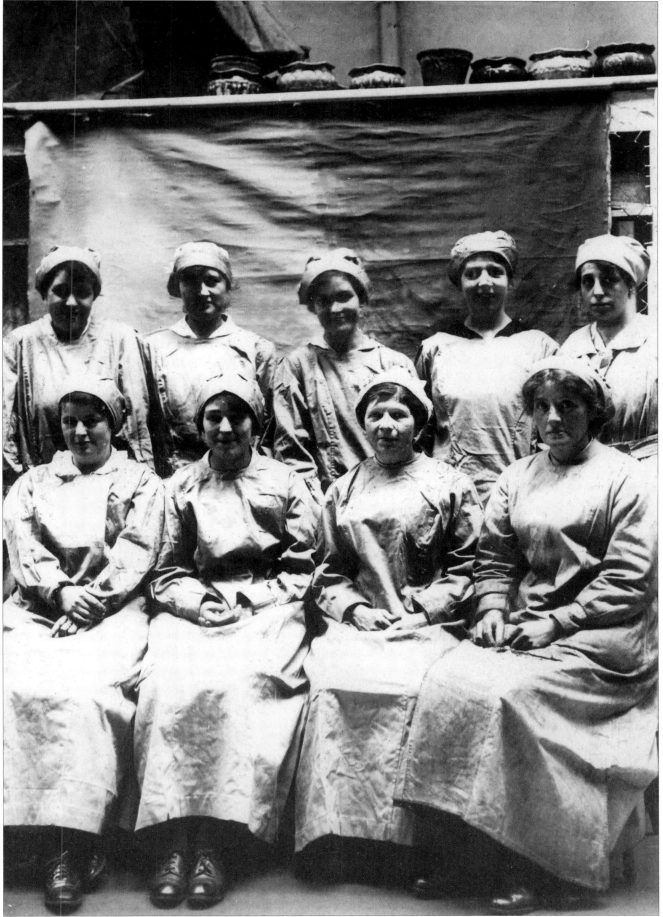

World War One women munitions workers.

Legendary
Captain Noel
Chavasse,
Liverpool's
greatest hero.
Medical officer
with the 10th
Battalion,
Liverpool
Scottish, in World
War One, he was
awarded the
Victoria Cross
twice - the latter
posthumously.

These battle-scarred, troop-carrying Mersey
ferryboats are the Iris (right)_ and the Daffodil,
on their return to the Mersey from Zeebrugge
in 1918. Each was given the prefix Royal - by
command of the king.

Parade of the 'Old Contemptibles' in November 1921, before attending a special church service for ex-servicemen.

Thousands of citizens witnessed the unveiling of Liverpool's fine new Cenotaph by Lord Derby on Armistice Day, 11 November 1930 - 12 years after the Great War 'to end wars'.

Merseyside at War – 1939-45

The Merseyside sea tragedy which, on 1 June 1939, seemed to herald the approaching war. New Birkenhead built submarine Thetis, on trials in Liverpool Bay, failed to surface when she became partly flooded. Although her stern showed above water at low-tide, rescue operations failed and only four of her complement managed to escape. Ninety-nine perished.

Liverpool's early air raid defences show some of the sandbagged city buildings as they looked in September 1939 - 17 days after war was declared.

Clutching their small possessions and carrying those ever-ready, boxed gas-masks, these Liverpool children bid farewell to their parents and homes and join the mass evacuation to 'safe' areas.

What a gas! Yes, many cars actually ran on coal gas. This was Liverpool's first car to be adapted. (September 1939).

The 'Phoney War' over, the Luftwaffe struck in earnest. Among the numerous raids on Merseyside, the first of the heaviest was the Christmas Blitz of 1940. But the most memorable and terrifying was that called the May Blitz, of 1941 - seven consecutive nights of heavy bombing that tore the heart out of the city's centre. On Merseyside (Liverpool, Bootle, Birkenhead and Wallasey, in particular), almost 4,000 people were killed, 3,500 seriously injured and thousands more slightly injured. Property damage was incalculable and the service and gallantry of firefighters, police, wardens and all those engaged in civil defence, beyond praise. The fearful damage and desolation caused by high-explosive and incendiary bombs to this central area is recorded in this dramatic photograph.

Not even the churches were sacrosanct when the rain-of-death fell on all and sundry. Liverpool's long-established 'Sailors' Church' of Our Lady and St Nicholas was destroyed by fire. It was later rebuilt.

A row of homes in Livingstone Street, Birkenhead, reduced to rubble . . .a common sight.

Ancient Egyptian relics survived for thousands of years, only to be destroyed or severely damaged in one night's air raid on
Liverpool. Destruction of the William Brown Street Museum.

Demolition workers await that ever-welcome 'cuppa' served by the 'Angels of the Air Raids' - the good ladies of the Women's Voluntary Service. (Twelve of the latter were killed in a bombed church hall in May 1941).

The Durning Road-Clint Road site of the worst British civilian incident of the war. Hundreds were sheltering in the basement of Edge Hill Training College when it received a direct hit by a parachute mine in November 1940. Whole families were among the 166 killed and many more were injured.

Merseyside's heroic fire-fighters - and often, scores more from other brigades summoned by a regional call - were always in the midst of danger and death as they fought innumerable fires during the bombing.

Mick, the pooch, orphaned when his owners were lost in the blitz, wisely made friends with the lads at Arnot Street Fire Station. As their mascot, he received his own NFS badge and identity tag - plus board and keep!

In spite of the Battle of the Atlantic and bombing of the port, Merseyside kept the convoys moving. No fewer than 1,285 arrived in Liverpool during the war. Vital Allied war materials, like the tank pictured, were unloaded.

Winston Churchill salutes Merseyside dockers in his 'hustle' tour of the city and port in April 1941, only days before the great May Blitz.

Mrs Eleanor Roosevelt in her 'hello troops' tour through massive Stanley Dock tobacco warehouse, taken over by the United States Army. (November 1942).

Thousands of Allied servicemen and women, stationed in Britain, visited or worked on wartime Merseyside. The vast US Army base at Burtonwood was only a few miles from Liverpool - their chief centre for entertainment. Many famous stars of stage and screen also visited them - like Jeanette McDonald, pictured here.

Thousands throng Lime Street to see the last Home Guard parade through the city in December 1944 before their stand-down.

Joyful crowds assemble on St George's Plateau and around the Cenotaph to celebrate the Allied victory.

The Battle of the Atlantic

An original wartime picture showing the plot and operations room of the Western Approaches combined headquarters in Derby House, Liverpool - the top-secret 'nerve-centre' for Allied operations in the Battle of the Atlantic from February 1941, until the end of the war. This historic centre, restored and named 'Western Approaches', is a big tourist attraction.

Portrait of a hero Captain Frederick John (Johnny) Walker, RN, CB, DSO and two bars, was called 'U-boat Killer No.1'. The Admiralty actually stated that he 'more than any other won the Battle of the Atlantic'. Walker's Second Escort Group sank six U-boats on one assignment and, on a previous patrol, sank three in six hours. Exhausted from over-work, he suffered a stroke and died in Liverpool, aged only 47.

Captain Walker and some of his gallant men at action stations in their relentless pursuit of U-boats.

Merseyside men are among this proud company of HMS Fame, part of an escort group of destroyers which hounded the
enemy.

Having surrendered to the Allies following the end of the war in Europe, submarine U.532, carrying cargo from Japan to Germany, is escorted into Gladstone Dock at Liverpool by the frigate HMS Grindall.

Tattered naval battle ensigns proudly enshrined in Bootle Town Hall's Council Chamber.

Admiral of the Fleet, Earl Mountbatten stands with the Lord Mayor of Liverpool, Mrs Ethel Wormald, and high-ranking officers, on the steps of Liverpool Cathedral on 4 May 1968. They watched a naval march-past to commemorate the 25th anniversary of the turning point of the Battle of the Atlantic.

A sea-war veteran courteously doffs his bowler to his Queen during one of the ceremonies on Merseyside commemorating the 50th anniversary of the Battle of the Atlantic.

Prince Charles and Princess Diana leaving Liverpool Anglican Cathedral after the Battle of the Atlantic service.

What's this? A U-boat in the Mersey and the Royal Yacht at Liverpool Landing Stage! Just part of Merseyside's Battle of
the Atlantic events, of course!

Prince Philip (in the Royal Yacht with flags flying) reviews the Fleet off Anglesey in really stormy weather.

Cheers and applause greet veterans of the Battle of the Atlantic, once more 'on parade'.

Strikes and Riots

That which is remembered in Liverpool as Red (or, generally, Bloody) Sunday, took place during the transport workers' strike and riots of 1911, when two men were shot and others, including prisoners, injured. This picture shows a military escort for a prison van in Scotland Road on 17 August 1911. Note tail-back of cage-front tramcars.

City shops are boarded up during the Police strike in 1919. But some policemen and many shoppers are still present in London Road.

Police Events of Yesterday

Lord Derby, as Lord Lieutenant of Lancashire, inspects detachments of Liverpool Police and Lancashire Constabulary and presents some medals at his Knowsley estate in July 1951.

Calling all cars . . .Councillor E.J.Dean, chairman of the Liverpool Watch Committee, opens the new police radio station at Allerton in April 1938.

By March 1930, all the Liverpool police point-duty men were equipped with this 'dustbin' type of protection box.

One of the highly-disciplined police horses gallops fearlessly through a ring of fire as Liverpool Mounted Police stage a 'Cossack' show.

Some of the thousand uniformed and plain-clothed policemen leaving Liverpool Cathedral in September 1966, when, in common with other forces, they attended a memorial service for three men of the Metropolitan Force who were shot dead.

A sporty Lagonda (capable of 90mph) for these Liverpool policemen in November 1937.

Around the Docks

Gladstone Dock, at the north end of the river, accommodated some of the biggest ships of the Mersey.

Part of the thriving Royal Seaforth Docks at the Mersey estuary, where one of the world's finest dock complexes incorporating container, grain and timber terminals, was created from 350 acres of reclaimed land.

Liverpool's South Docks in 1971, before the massive redevelopment changes. Ship, right, lies alongside the now-demolished Brunswick Dock grain silo.

This was Coburg Dock, now converted into a popular grand marina, often used by visiting boats.

Birkenhead's West and East Float Docks, as they appeared in August 1977.

Unloading Russian timber at up-river Garston Docks.

Pier Head and Landing Stage

These three magnificent buildings gracing the Pier Head are (left to right): Royal Liver, Cunard and Port of Liverpool. This delightful waterfront afforded millions of liner passengers their first close-up of England when their ships tied up at Liverpool Landing Stage.

Liverpool's former landing stage was a 2,500ft long floating platform of wooden decking on iron pontoons and carried a superstructure of sheds, offices, shelters, gangways and other facilities - all of which rose and fell with the tides. The ferry boats tied up at the section known as George's Stage and the liners and bigger vessels berthed at the adjoining Prince's Stage. It was a wonder of the world! The picture shows Prince's Stage in the 1960s, with Riverside Station and Prince's Dock behind.

Vehicles at the Pier Head in August 1932, queuing to go down the 'Floating roadway' (right) and cross the Mersey by 'luggage' boats before the Queensway tunnel was opened.

A high tide levels off the hinged floating roadway, which stretched from St Nicholas Place to Prince's Landing Stage.

Roofed Prince's Parade: Riverside Station in its heyday was on the right and access to Prince's Landing Stage, Customs, waiting rooms, etc., was on the left.

Riverside Station where the boat-trains from London arrived and departed.

12 June 1895, and the White Star liner, Germanic, dressed overall, prepares to sail from Liverpool to New York with the
first passengers to arrive at the nearby Riverside Station, inaugurated that day.

Strike-bound Dublin and Belfast boats lie idle in Prince's Dock, behind Riverside Station.

Demolition of the old landing stage nears completion. Royal Daffodil alongside.

Passenger bridges, great girders and massive chains kept the landing stage securely tied to the mainland wall.

Tugs fight to stabilise Liverpool's new and much smaller concrete floating landing stage, battered by gales after its installation.

This was Prince's Parade in July 1962, with another long queue for the popular Isle of Man steamers.

Luckier holidaymakers manage to get a seat in the huge waiting room.

Motor cyclists from all over Britain converge on Liverpool to sail to the Isle of Man when the TT Races are being held.

All aboard a North Wales steamer for another invigorating trip to delightful places like Llandudno and the Menai Straits. Manx steamer, King Orry (astern) prepares for her island holidaymakers.

The Mersey Tunnels

An historic scene, lit by gas and candlelight, that depicts the Beaumont boring machine having broken down the last barrier of rock for the Mersey Railway Tunnel to join Liverpool with Birkenhead in 1884. Steam trains (choking passengers and staff with fumes) ran on this railway, formally opened by King Edward VII, then Prince of Wales, in 1886 until May 1903, when electric trains took over.

A similar, wet 'holing-through' ceremony in Queensway (road) Tunnel on 3 April 1928, when the Lord Mayor of Liverpool, Miss Margaret Beavan, greeted Birkenhead's Mayor, Alderman F.Naylor. Sir Archibald Salvidge, with pickaxe, made the initial break-through.

Excavating the lower half of the Queensway Tunnel in September 1929, with a suspended roadway used for transferring material.

The Duke of York, who became King George VI, inspects the tunnel workings with Sir Thomas White. But how long will that gleaming shine on the Duke's shoes last?

Below: Queensway's Birkenhead junction chamber in October 1933. The dock branch tunnel is on the right.

The vast fresh air duct in the lower part of Queensway Tunnel, under land, pictured in November 1930.

Traffic tests being made in March 1932, for the new tunnel entrance at Liverpool. Vehicles line up at temporary pay-boxes.

A personal historic picture for thousands of Merseysiders who walked through the Queensway Tunnel when it was first opened to the public on Sunday, 17 December 1933, each person paying 6d for the privilege!

The Royal car about to enter the new Queensway Tunnel, watched by a crowd estimated at about 200,000.

18 July 1934, and King George V presses a button to operate the curtains covering the Tunnel entrance and declare
Queensway open.

A floodlit scene of night-building activity at the twin tubes of the Kingsway Tunnel - generally known as the Wallasey Tunnel.

Queen Elizabeth opens the Kingsway Tunnel in June 1971. All ranks at attention as the Queen's Colour of the King's (Liverpool) regiment is held aloft.

Railways and Stations

Liverpool established the first 'real', long-distance railway in the world, with commercial passenger and freight trains run entirely by mechanical traction. This was the Liverpool and Manchester Railway, built by engineer George Stephenson and his team and it was copied elsewhere from then on. The opening, on 15 September 1830, by the Duke of Wellington, was a grand affair with lots of festivities, marred only by the tragic death of Liverpool MP, William Huskisson, who was run over by the historical locomotive, the Rocket.

Liverpool's suburban Broadgreen Station, on the Liverpool-Manchester line, photographed in 1865.

This ancient locomotive, the Lion, dating from 1838, is still preserved in excellent condition as a museum piece. It is seen here, pulling coaches, as the chief exhibit for the Liverpool celebration of the centenary of the Liverpool and Manchester Railway, in September 1930, when a big pageant was held on Wavertree Playground.

This civic group is standing before the world's first passenger railway tunnel, part of the Liverpool and Manchester Railway, in September 1925, the anniversary of the Stockton and Darlington Railway. Girl with the wreath is Miss May Wotton, Railway Centenary Queen.

The Northumbrian and performers at the Wavertree pageant.

A great public send-off for this Stanier Black Five 45110, on a special farewell excursion as (appropriately) the last main line steam train to leave Lime Street Station, in August 1968.

Summertime always saw crowds at Exchange Station (the general route to the North), like these queuing for Southport trains in June 1967.

'High-level' Central Station in July 1971. Below this was the long-established underground railway station, known as Central low-level, now a major station in the Merseyside network.

But where have all the commuters gone now . . .? Exchange Station, in August 1978, disused and ready for demolition since the 'underground' opened in 1977.

Demolition of the high-level Central Station for inner-city redevelopment.

Merseyside's extensive electric rail system, partly underground and linking stations as far apart as West Kirby, Southport and Ormskirk.

The great brick cavern of James Street Station before modernisation.

Even Queen Elizabeth
travelled by public transport
in this special 'royal' train,
taking her from Liverpool to
Kirkby during her Merseyside
visit in October 1978.

A farewell tour for
railway enthusiasts
in April 1985,
after BR Class 503
trains on the
Wirral electric
railway system
were withdrawn
from general
service to be
replaced by more
modern stock.

Liverpool Overhead Railway

Liverpool Overhead Railway provided a vital waterfront service and, as a Victorian project for alleviating dockland road traffic congestion, was a very modern concept. The 'Ovee' or 'Dockers' Umbrella' (sheltering dock workers walking below it from the rain) was opened on 6 March 1893, and closed at the end of 1956.

Sketch of the formal opening of the Liverpool Overhead Railway in February 1893. This was at the Pier Head Station. Note the sailing ship masts in George's Dock (right).

One of the original overhead coaches, laid up at North Mersey Goods Station, pictured in June 1961.

Last tickets to ride! Some of the hundreds of Overhead Railway enthusiasts, who boarded the trains on the last day of their public operation, 30 December 1956.

The last Overhead train leaving Seaforth to make the final round trip to Dingle and back.

A number of sections of the Overhead Railway were wrecked in air raids. This scene was in Wapping, part of the dock road.

But bombers could not be blamed for this! The Pier Head Station starts to disappear under the demolition hammers at Christmas time, 1957.

Tramcars and Buses

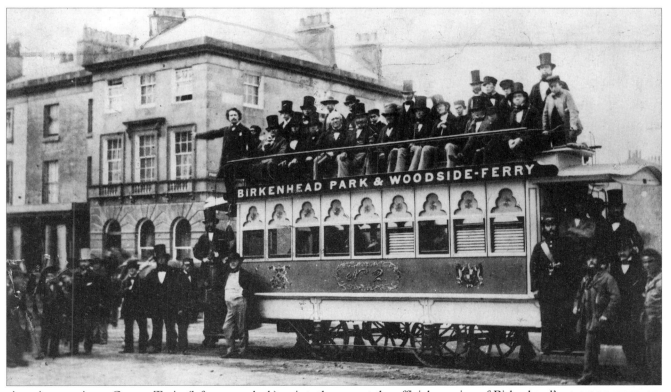

American engineer George Train (left, upper deck) points the way at the official opening of Birkenhead's street tramway on 30 August 1860. Other towns soon copied his sensible idea.

An open-top 'garden seat' horse tram on the Seaforth-Pier Head route, pictured in Derby Road, Bootle, in May 1894.

The Pier Head was Liverpool's chief tramcar terminus. Here, old 'toast rack' trams pass a horse-cab rank, with the busy Overhead Railway running parallel with the dock road. St Nicholas' Church is on the left and Tower Building, right.

A fresh-air tram heads townwards past Five Lamps, Waterloo.

66 tramcars were totally destroyed in the disastrous fire at Green Lane depot on 8 November 1947.

Parade of 13 Liverpool 'last trams' in Lime Street, on 14 September 1957. A band at their Pier Head start played 'Auld Lang Syne'!

Long-serving driver and conductor of the last tram, Mr. T. Webster and Mr G. Rodden.

The official last tram (No.293) being shipped out to Boston from Gladstone Dock, bound for the Trolley Museum at Kennebunk Port.

Birkenhead's last tramcar, dressed for the occasion, is given a civic send-off on its final journey on 17 July 1937.

Crowds would gather in Liverpool's main streets on the special occasions when the Illuminated Tramcar, with top-deck band, toured the city. This tram is in Utting Avenue, Anfield, in the 1930s.

The Pier Head tram terminus with some of the great Liverpool liners on the river. Note New Brighton Tower (top right).

When the buses took over . . .Pier Head bus terminus in September 1961.

Trams gone, Liverpool is now a bus-busy city.

Atlantean buses in their Liverpool depot.

Queuing for the
buses has no
meaning when a
crowd starts
pushing for
places!

Line-up of eight 'clippies' in April 1956, when 500 women helped 'man' the Liverpool fleet of 1,100 buses and trams and
added a spot of glamour to the city's public transport.

Ferries Across the Mersey

Chapter House of Birkenhead Priory, dating from about 1150. Its Benedictine monks were granted the rights to operate the first regular Mersey ferry service.

Queuing on George's Landing Stage to cross the Mersey by steam ferry in about 1886.

A Birkenhead paddle ferry beats her way through ice-floes on the Mersey in the big freeze of a late Victorian winter. People could walk on ice across the river from bank to bank!

Pullman rail cars for Ireland being loaded on to the old Oxton 'luggage' boat at Birkenhead's West Float in the 1920s.

This is how George's Landing Stage used to look when a sunny post-war holiday brought thousands of trippers there to board the ferries to Seacombe and New Brighton.

Oh, the joy of a river ferry trip! An educational cruise on the Royal Daffodil in 1974.

New ferryboat, the Mountwood (left) with the Claughton, joins the Birkenhead fleet in January 1960.

Left: Seacombe landing stage's fog-bell, reconditioned and repositioned in August 1931. Right: A Wallasey ferries' engineer inspects Royal Daffodil's stern as she lies beached on the riverside.

Royal Daffodil noses into her George's stage berth.

Inspection of past and present Royal Marines at Prince's Landing Stage in April 1955, for their annual commemoration of the anniversary of the landings at Zeebrugge on St George's Day, 1918, when the Mersey ferries Iris and Daffodil played vital roles as troopships.

Liverpool Airport

An historic picture of Liverpool Airport, at Speke, in its formative days (*c.*1933), with a twin-engined De Havilland 86 beside the humble farmhouse, which then acted as the flying-control building. The site originally was selected for the Corporation by pioneer aviator Sir Alan Cobham, of flying-circus fame. Today, Liverpool Airport provides first rate passenger and freight facilities, with a huge, riverside runway capable of serving the needs of the largest and fastest aircraft. Future plans include a new terminal, roads and car-parks, all based on a one-runway operation.

Liverpool Airport's present terminal building.

An educational 'flip' for 70 pupils of Deyes Lane C.S.School, Maghull, about to board a Cambrian Viscount for a flight to Carlisle and back in October 1971.

Another exciting 'outdoor lesson' at the airport for these bright little youngsters from Merchant Taylor's Girls' School.

While hundreds of folk gathered to see this monstrous USAF Galaxy transport aircraft, this proud little girl put on a show all of her own!

The terminal building verandahs were always ideal spots for 'watching all the planes go by'. (July 1968).

Liverpool's Two Great Cathedrals

Liverpool is the proud possessor of two great Cathedrals - the Liverpool Cathedral Church of Christ, founded in 1904 and now generally known as the Anglican Cathedral, and the Roman Catholic Metropolitan Cathedral of Christ The King, founded in 1933.

The Anglican Cathedral, a massive sandstone Gothic structure, rising 500 feet above the Mersey and the last of Britain's cathedrals, was designed by Roman Catholic architect Sir Giles Gilbert Scott, 'to last a thousand years'.

Only a few hundred yards away at the end of a straight, linked street called Hope, stands the ultra-modern Metropolitan Cathedral.

This was designed originally by architect Sir Edwin Lutyens, who envisaged the world's biggest cathedral, but the plan was abandoned on financial grounds after the completion of the crypt in October 1958. Architect Sir Frederick Gibberd, a Free Churchman, created the present beautiful building over the crypt.

With the formal completion of the Anglican Cathedral in 1978, and that of the Metropolitan Cathedral in 1967, both magnificent edifices attract world-wide attention. What is more, they are symbolic of Christian unity - so evident on Merseyside.

The mighty Anglican Cathedral (still being built in this picture), rises above St James's Cemetery, where many famous old Liverpool personalities are buried.

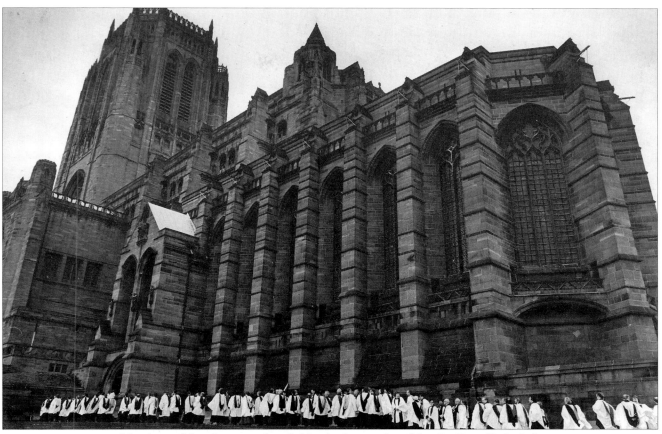

Members of the clergy are dwarfed by the immensity of the Anglican Cathedral.

Rare photograph of King Edward VII and Queen Alexandra at the Cathedral's foundation-stone laying ceremony by the King in July 1904. The day was declared a holiday and Liverpool was *en fête* in perfect summer weather. Streets were decorated, 15,000 children sang the National Anthem, and a large amphitheatre filled with dignitaries surrounded the Royal dais. The stone was dedicated by the Archbishop of York.

Cathedral builders . . . many of the stone masons and wood-carvers spent most of their lives working on this cathedral, which took 74 years to complete.

An example of the intricate carved stonework in the Cathedral is shown in the Rankin Porch, being built here in 1938.

Queen Elizabeth attends the dedication service on 25 October 1978, to mark the formal completion of the Cathedral in the presence of Archbishop Stuart Blanch, the Archbishop of York, the Rt Revd David Sheppard, Bishop of Liverpool, and many VIPs.

Lord Mayor of Liverpool (Councillor Ruth Dean) and city officials look on as the Queen signs the visitors' book at Liverpool Town Hall.

Birth of a fine Cathedral . . .80,000 people gathered on Whit Monday, 5 June 1933, for the Metropolitan Cathedral's foundation ceremony, conducted by Dr Richard Downey, Archbishop of Liverpool, in the presence of the Papal Legate, Cardinal MacRory.

On 16 October 1980, some 2,000 people attended a memorial service at the Cathedral to the 44 crew who died when the Liverpool-owned bulk-carrier, Derbyshire, sank in a typhoon off Japan the previous month.

A Brownlow Hill site was bought in 1930 for the building of the Cathedral and work was begun on the crypt, completed after the war. With the original grand project then abandoned for lack of funds, an entirely different Cathedral, very modern in concept, was built over these vaults, pictured under construction in October 1938.

Taking shape at an advanced stage in May 1966, the 'Metro' proudly raises skywards its lovely lantern tower of stained glass. The powerful steel and concrete 'legs' of the mainframe stand braced to carry this magnificent 2,000-ton crown, which produces remarkable changes of colour and light as the sun crosses the heavens.

The Metropolitan Cathedral, now a well-established, impressive city landmark.

Pistol-packing resident architect, Philip Harrison tests the Cathedral's acoustics in April 1967.

Bishop Augustine Harris, Auxiliary Bishop of Liverpool, about to give the symbolic knock on the Cathedral's main doors.

The consecration of the completed Cathedral, on 14 May 1967, was a solemn yet jubilant occasion. Thousands of people filled the Cathedral, the Philharmonic Hall, where the ceremony was watched through closed circuit television, and gathered outside the Cathedral, where the service was relayed by loudspeakers. Among those present was the Duke of Norfolk, representing the Queen, Cardinal John Heenan, the Papal Legate, three other cardinals, 52 bishops, Prime Minister Harold Wilson, the Prime Minister of the Republic of Ireland, Jack Lynch and Edward Heath, Leader of the Opposition.

Firm friends . . .
Archbishop Derek
Warlock and Bishop
David Sheppard in
Hope Street.

The Pope Pays a Visit

An historic and
emotional moment as the
Pope, making his first
call at the Anglican
Cathedral, is greeted by
Bishop David Sheppard
and both embrace.

Scores of thousands of people of many religions lined the city route taken by Pope John Paul when he visited Liverpool in May 1982, and went 'rideabout' in his special 'Popemobile,' smiling, waving and blessing. This highway between the two Cathedrals is well-named Hope Street.

A packed congregation in the Anglican Cathedral (and the city in general) warmly welcomed this humble but great and wonderful contribution towards Christian unity. The Pope later wore his full regalia.

Jubilant crowds, estimated at 150,000, awaited the Pontiff's arrival at the Metropolitan Cathedral to rousing cheers and waving arms.

A Papal blessing for
a little lady.

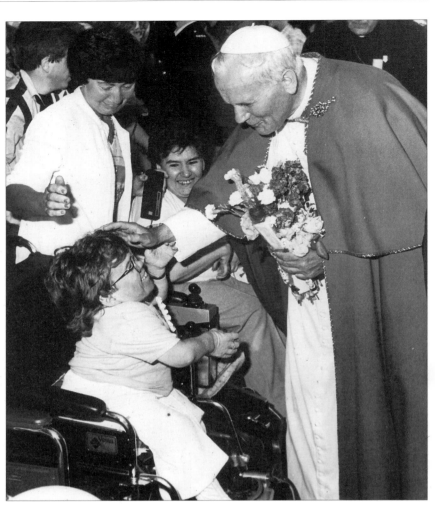

Farewell to Liverpool by
the Pilgrim of Peace.

Royal Events Recalled

Wind and blinding rain failed to prevent Liverpool's loyal citizens from turning out in their thousands to welcome Queen Victoria on her visit to the city in May 1886 - in an open carriage, too!

The Duke of York, who became King George V, laying the foundation stone of the Liverpool General Post Office, Victoria Street, on 10 September 1894.

Water Street, gaily decorated for the Coronation of King Edward VII, in 1902.

Close-up of a popular Royal couple. King George V and Queen Mary toured the city in an open carriage when they came
for the consecration of Liverpool Cathedral in July 1924.

Prince George opens the reconstructed Walker Art Gallery on 4 October 1933. Lord Derby is seated extreme left of the Prince.

When Liverpool celebrated King George VI's Coronation in 1937, the whole city was decorated and countless street parties for children were held. Even the city's large fish market made a brave show!

Massive crowds gathered in Castle Street by the Town Hall for the finale of Liverpool's Coronation festivities, broadcast in 1937 (and photographed through overhead tram wires!)

Floral crown for 'Peter Pan', in Sefton Park, from Liverpool's Lady Mayoress during the Coronation Week celebrations in May 1937.

Thousands of Liverpool schoolchildren were presented with souvenir Coronation certificates and medals in 1937. Here the Lady Mayoress makes presentations at Birchfield Road School.

Hundreds of proud youngsters who presented their 1937 Coronation physical culture display at New Brighton open-air pool.

The Earl of Shrewsbury opens the Coronation decorations at Priory Buildings, Birkenhead, in May 1937.

Members of Bootle's W.V.S.Darby and Joan Club enjoy a 1953 Coronation celebration meal and concert at Bootle Town Hall.

More than 3,000 people packed Liverpool Stadium to hear the 1953 Coronation Concert given by the Liverpool Philharmonic Orchestra (conductor Hugo Rignold) and the Philharmonic and Liverpool Welsh Choral Union choirs.

Big thrill for the neighbours when the Queen Mother, with Liverpool City Council officials, visited a Council house in Speke, in June 1957, while in Liverpool for the City's Charter celebrations.

After a busy day in Liverpool in June 1971, when she opened the Kingsway Tunnel, Queen Elizabeth relaxed at the Royal
Variety Show at the Empire Theatre. Here, in all her jewelled finery, she is introduced to impresario Sir Bernard Delfont
and the artists by the Lord Mayor, Alderman Charles Cowlin.

Sunny smiles on the sunny day of 21 June 1977, when the Queen made her Silver Jubilee visit to Merseyside, accompanied by the Duke of Edinburgh.

Dunluce Street, Walton - one of the numerous streets which celebrated the Silver Jubilee with outdoor parties

Great Ships of the Mersey

Hundreds of Britain's finest ships once sailed from the Mersey, carrying Merseyside crews to the farthest corners of the world. And Merseyside was so proud of them all, particularly the famous liners, symbolising the romance of luxury sea travel.

World-famous personalities, including royalty, statesmen, business tycoons and film stars, regularly arrived at Liverpool from America and Canada via Cunard, White Star and Canadian Pacific ships.

It was to India via Anchor Line and with elder Dempster to West Africa. South America was linked through the liners of Pacific Steam Navigation, and the little Booth Liners also carried many an explorer, adventurer and author to the jungles of the Amazon.

Fleets of cargo vessels once crowded the busy port, where the docks were full of not only British ships but others representing the maritime nations of the world.

Smaller coastal ships, the Manx, Irish and Welsh boats, the cross-river ferries, tugs and umpteen other vessels, down to floating cranes and barges, also played their parts in some fascinating river scenes.

Young and old emigrants in the early 1870s, stand apprehensively on Prince's Landing Stage with their meagre possessions. The river looks busy with small paddle steamers; an Isle of Man boat is tied up (left) and a large steam-sail liner lies in mid-river.

The sailing ships of James Baines' famous Black Ball Line could reach Australia in about nine weeks and it took some 35 years for the steamers to catch up with their records! Here, returning to the Mersey from Melbourne, is the Marco Polo (commanded by Captain 'Bully' Forbes) declaring herself 'The Fastest Ship in the world'.

White Star Line's Oceanic (1) made passenger-liner history as the first of the 'luxury' liners. Her maiden voyage from Liverpool to New York was on 2 March 1871.

Great Eastern, engineer I.K.Brunel's 19,000-ton, five-funnelled, six-masted ship, was the largest vessel in the world during her lifetime. A bit of a 'white elephant' liner, she sailed from Liverpool to America many times and also served as a cable ship. She became an exhibition ship for Lewis's Stores in 1886 and was broken up at Birkenhead in 1888.

Berengaria, formerly the German liner Imperator, which went to Cunard as a suitable war reparation for the loss of the Lusitania.

Fabulous Mauretania (I), which many folk still regard as the best-loved British liner of all time, makes an attractive picture in her white cruising livery. She and her ill-fated sister, Lusitania, were both 'Speed Queens of the North Atlantic' in their day.

Picturesquely framed is the old Cunarder, Ascania, arriving at Liverpool from New York in December 1954. The bow on the left belongs to the Booth Liner, Hildebrand, newly arrived from South America.

The new Mauretania (II) leaving Gladstone Lock for her trails in the Firth of Clyde. At 35,738 tons, this Birkenhead-built liner was the largest ship to be constructed in England.

Mighty Mauretania
makes an impressive
sight, undergoing an
overhaul in Gladstone
Graving Dock.

Last of the White Star Liners, Britannic III,
taken over by Cunard, was one of the most
popular ships of the Mersey, sailing
regularly from Liverpool to New York.

Magnificent Empress of Scotland, flagship of Canadian Pacific's fleet, leaving Montreal for Liverpool in May 1952.

One of the renowned 'White Empresses', Canadian Pacific's former Duchess of Richmond, renamed Empress of Canada II, as she looked before the fire which destroyed her in Gladstone Dock, in January 1953.

Thick steel hawsers take the strain to winch the burned-out liner upright before she was refloated, towed away and scrapped.

Sylvania, last of Cunard's 'sparkling quartette' of 22,000-ton luxury passenger liners, which once made regular transatlantic passages from Liverpool. Her last scheduled voyage from the port on 24 November 1966, marked the end of the regular passenger service that had existed between Liverpool and New York for 120 years.

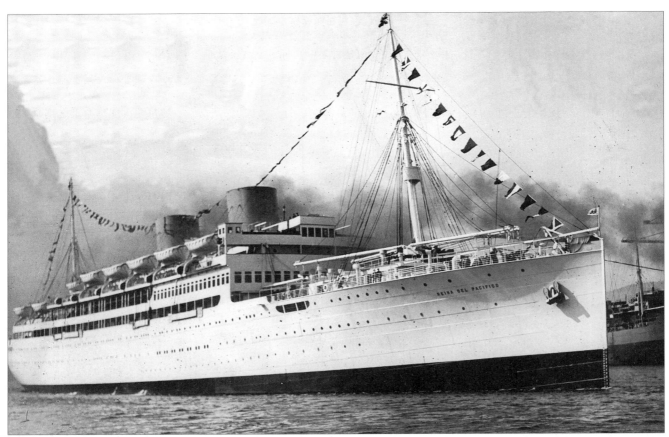

Pacific Steam Navigation Company's fine new motorship, Reina Del Pacifico, on her first visit to Liverpool in March 1931, to become one of the established favourite Liverpool liners on the South America service.

Elder Dempster's Aureol was the last regular large passenger liner to operate from Liverpool and her sailing from the port to West Africa on 16 March 1972, ended the wonderful era of Merseyside's liners.

Cammell Laird, Shipbuilders to the World

One of the biggest industrial calamities to strike Merseyside was the closure of the great shipyard of Cammell Laird, Birkenhead, established in 1828. The company's fine building record (so vital during the wars), included the two Ark Royal aircraft carriers (1938 and 1955), the battleship Prince of Wales, and the luxury liner Mauretania the second.

Craftsmen at work in Laird's joinery shop.

Men with 'iron muscles' aid this hydraulic hammer in shaping a ship's steel plate.

Scousers might say that 'this is the gear'! Actually, it's the giant 6½-ton auxiliary timing wheel, which was fitted to the main casing of Mauretania's engines.

Launching of the gigantic Laird's-built oil rig, Sovereign Explorer.

" . . .the most wonderful launch I have ever seen," said Queen Elizabeth (now Queen Mother), naming HMS Ark Royal at Cammell Laird's shipyard in 1950. The 38,000-ton giant was the largest vessel built by Laird's who, in 1938, had also constructed the former aircraft carrier of that name, which was sunk in World War Two.

Down the slipway glides Ark Royal, but unable to begin her career until completion in 1955.

The sun goes down on a once-mighty shipyard - hopefully, not for good!

Albert Dock —
A Tourist Magnet

One of the finest projects undertaken on Merseyside was the restoration of square Albert Dock and its surrounding warehouses, silted up and derelict for years. The complex, now a major attraction for visitors, incorporates a 'village' of specialist shops, restaurants, pubs, offices, the Merseyside Maritime Museum, the Tate of the North Gallery and a Granada TV studio.

Front view of the Albert Dock warehouses, built like a massive fortress, with Canning Dock in the foreground.

A prime example of the restoration work: The ruined piermaster's house and demolished bridge at Albert Dock during the years of decay.

A real glimpse of the past after restoration.

The bare brick, stone and iron of these former mighty warehouses create an impressive contrast with the modern shops and other facilities within the 'village'.

Merseyside Maritime Museum, situated on a prime riverside site at the Albert Dock, is now one of the world's best.

Prince Albert officially opened the Albert Dock and warehouses and now, 142 years later, Prince Charles reopens this vast, historic complex.

QE2 Pays Homage to Liverpool

One of the most moving modern maritime chapters of Merseyside was written on the glorious, warm summer day of 24 July 1990, when the Queen Elizabeth II came to Liverpool.

The magnificent liner, here to celebrate Cunard's 150th anniversary, was the first of the giant 'Queens' to sail into the Mersey. A proud 'homecoming', too, for Captain Robin Woodall, who lives at Hoylake, Wirral.

Thousands of excited sightseers line both banks of the river and those on ferries and numerous small craft took a closer look as she rode at anchor before the Pier Head (and the Cunard Building, where the company had its headquarters).

Sadly, here for but a day, QE2 was serenaded by massed 'choirs' of spectators on either bank as darkness fell, with music and song also pouring forth from the liner's public-address system.

With broadcast thanks to all from her Captain, and three great blasts of her whistle, QE2 departed.

It was like old times to see a great liner in the Mersey again.

The huge liner pays homage to the port where her world-famous line began.

A young generation gets its first sight of a luxury liner on Merseyside.

A grand display of fireworks honoured the 'Queen' on her late-evening departure.

Tall Ships Turn Back the Clock

The visits of many beautiful international sailing ships to the Mersey on the two occasions of the Tall Ships' Race, stirred Merseyside's deep maritime roots and pride.

They brought to life a bygone era of the port's rich and mighty past and, on their first visit, in 1984, more than a million people on both sides of the river, were drawn to the waterfronts for this grand, picturesque spectacle, lasting four fun-filled days.

Their departure, saluting the Queen on the Royal Yacht, was sorrowful. But Merseyside was happy to welcome their return in 1992 for the climax of the 500th anniversary of the Grand Regatta Columbus, celebrating the great navigator's historic transatlantic voyage.

Left: Public interest in the Tall Ships may be gauged from this scene at Vittoria Dock, Birkenhead, where many of the vessels were berthed.

A speedboat escorts Spain's lovely top-sail schooner, Juan Sebastian de Elcano, as she sails past the Pier Head. The King of Spain, accompanied by his Queen at the Liverpool reception, had served as a midshipman on this barquentine.

The giant Russian ship, Kruzenshtern, the biggest of the tall ships, under the watchful eyes of Liverpool's lofty Liver Birds, perched on the towers of the Royal Liver Building.

Thousands of Liverpool spectators gave a warm welcome to all the crews of the Tall Ships on their parade through the city.

Big smiles from the Royal yacht as the Queen, with Prince Andrew, watch the departure of the Tall Ships from the Mersey
in August 1984.

A 'yard-arm salute' from the crew of Colombia's glorious Arc Gloria as she leaves the Mersey.

Local, But Nationally Famous

Left: 'Kitty' Wilkinson, founder of the city's wash-houses. Born poor, in Londonderry, in 1786, she came to Liverpool and during the cholera outbreaks in 1832 and 1834, opened her backyard boiler room to neighbours to wash their clothing. Her valuable contribution to health in this respect, and her self-denial in other charitable public work, earned her an honoured place in Liverpool history. Thanks to her example, the Town Council built the first public wash-house in the country, in 1842, with Kitty and her husband as superintendents. The scheme was emulated by other towns.

Right: Doctor William Henry Duncan, Liverpool's (and Britain's) first Medical Officer of Health (1847-1863), who pioneered community health in Britain.

Steble Street wash-house, off Park Road, Toxteth, in about 1913.

Woodman, spare that tree! Liverpool-born Liberal, William Ewart Gladstone, four times Prime Minister.

Sir Harold Wilson, MP for Huyton, Liverpool . . .twice Prime Minister.

A city alderman, JP and Member of Parliament for Liverpool Exchange, and late Mrs Elizabeth ('Bessie') Braddock will long be remembered. 'Battling Bessie', as she was often called, readily agreed that she was a rebel. Loved and hated, she was a champion with her constituents and became nationally famous. She is pictured with film star Marlene Dietrich, after they had dined together in 1955.

Right: Liverpool lost a great character with the death of Arthur Dooley, who once worked as deckhand on tugboats and eventually became a brilliant and nationally-famous sculptor.

Far right: Liverpool-born Regimental Sergeant Major Ron Brittain, 36 years with the Coldstream Guards, boasted the loudest voice in the British Army.

Two Merseysiders who will always be associated with the early assaults on Mount Everest were the first two in the back row of this group - Andrew Irvine and George Leigh Mallory, both from Birkenhead, who were lost without trace in the mountains in June 1924.

Nicholas Monsarrat, Liverpool author of the best-seller, 'The Cruel Sea,' on a visit to his native city in April 1955

Some of Our Talented Entertainers

Above: Impressario Bill Kenwright and playwright Alan Bleasedale share a joke with Martin Shaw, star of their play, 'Are you Lonesome Tonight'.

Right: Arthur Askey at Rhyl, where, as a boy, he loved to watch the pierrot shows.

Far right: Tommy Handley, the well-loved star of radio's 'It's That Man Again' (I.T.M.A.) programme.

It's all jester a big joke for 'Chuckle Captain' comedian Ken Dodd and his jolly crew at this Runcorn launching of the Bridgewater Motor Boat Club's 'Halton Explorer'.

Cilla Black gets a golf lesson from comedian Jimmy Tarbuck (a fellow Liverpudlian) and the late Dickie Henderson.

Two Liverpool 'greats' - Ted Ray and Rob Wilton (centre) chat about old times.

The Beatles

A rare shot of the Beatles, on home ground - a bombed site in Liverpool.

And this is where it all began
. . .the world-famous
Cavern, in Mathew Street,
where the Beatles played.

John Lennon probably
would have had this
picture framed . . .
Yoko Ono and their
son, Sean, before the
Royal Liver Building
and its Liver Birds,
synonymous with
Lennon's birthplace.

Ringo conducts his son on a nostalgic tour of Mathew Street - a virtual shrine to the Beatles - and other of the foursome's old haunts.

Tommy Steele sculptured and presented to Liverpool this sad statue of 'Eleanor Rigby' as a tribute to the Beatles. (1982).

The Beatles are still one of Liverpool's main attractions - even as statues. Here, in December 1988, eight years after John's Lennon's death, Father McKenzie, made famous by the song 'Eleanor Rigby', pays homage at the cult-created 'shrine'.

Tens of thousands of fans gather at St George's Plateau for the John Lennon Vigil in December 1980.

Delighted Paul McCartney (proudly wearing a Liver Bird badge) acknowledges a big welcome at his first concert in Liverpool for 11 years - at King's Dock, on 28 June 1990.

A Few Theatres —
Past and Present

Liverpool has had many theatres and music halls, dating from the 18th century. This picture shows the demolition of the Old Empire Theatre (formerly the Alexandra Theatre) in Lime Street, in 1924.

The Empire Theatre as it is today, on the same site, with the 1879 Steble Fountain in the foreground.

Liverpool Playhouse, the city's ornate and oldest surviving theatre, where many famous actors and actresses began their careers. It was formerly the New Star Music hall, built in 1865. Foreground: 'Professor' Codman's Punch and Judy show has also been operating in the city for about one and quarter centuries!

The Bard himself surveys the tragedy of the death of Liverpool's lovely Shakespeare Theatre, destroyed by fire in March 1976, after its conversion to an elegant cabaret club.

The second Royal Court Theatre, opened in October 1938.

Our Soccer Mad City!

Merseyside and football are virtually synonymous! Supporters of Everton, Liverpool and rising Tranmere have few equals in enthusiasm. Here are some of the keen but sad, banner-bearing multitude in the old Liverpool Kop on the day of the last match before its closure for conversion to seating.

Never has a football manager inspired his team like the late, inimitable Bill Shankly. Football was his very life. His players and supporters idolised him and he built Liverpool into one of the most outstanding clubs in Europe. This picture shows 'Shanks', his team and the fans with the League Championship trophy, 1972-73.

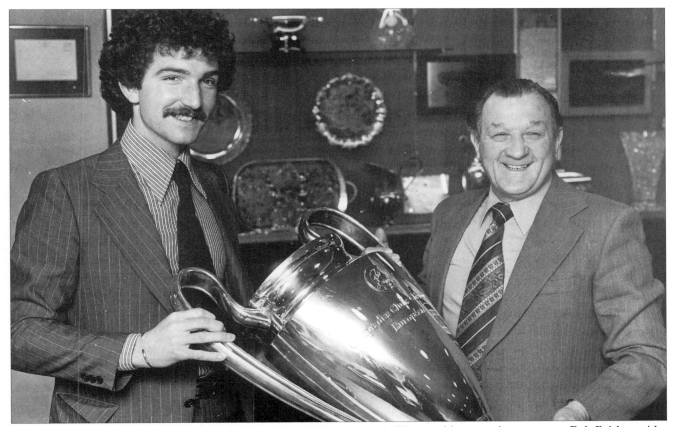

One of the most respected names in the history of football - popular, brilliant and long-serving manager, Bob Paisley, with new-signing Graeme Souness and the club's fabulous European Cup. Graeme, of course, eventually succeeded another superstar 'Kop hero,' Kenny Dalglish, who had become Liverpool's manager.

Scores of thousands of cheering people lined the city route taken by victorious Everton in 1933 when they returned with the FA Cup, held aloft by football's legendary idol, Dixie Dean.

Everton's 1969-70 League Championship side, pictured with the famous trophy.

Charity cap: Everton
chairman, the late
Sir John Moores
(centre), with Brian
Labone (left) and
Dixie Dean, showing
one of Brian's 16
international caps.
This raised £200 at
a special reception in
October 1972, to
launch a testimonial
fund for Labone.

Probably the biggest crowd that
ever assembled on Merseyside in
one spot - tens of thousands of
soccer-mad, cheering, singing
supporters (including many
Evertonians) welcomed home
Liverpool FC , with the UEFA
Cup in May 1973. Said manager
Bill Shankly: "This is the greatest
day of my career."

A picture that speaks for itself . . .The sea of floral tributes on the hallowed turf of Anfield following the terrible tragedy at Hillsborough on 15 April 1989, which resulted in 96 deaths.

The grand homecoming of popular Tranmere Rovers FC's team on 6 June 1991, after their 1-0 play-off win over Bolton to gain promotion to Division Two after more than half a century in exile in the lower divisions.

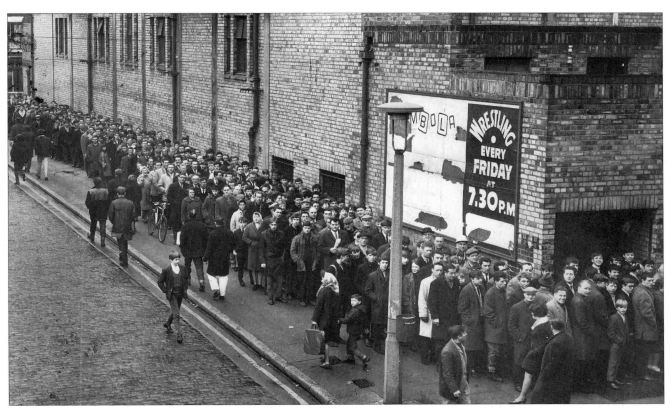

Thousands of football fans form a very long queue in February 1966, outside the old Liverpool Stadium for tickets for the Everton-Liverpool League 'derby' match on 19 March.

Aintree, Home of the Grand National

They're off! . . .A much better start to the 1994 Grand National at Aintree the world's greatest steeplechase, than in the previous year, with its dramatic starting problems.

Legendary Red Rum, thrice winner of the National and twice second, has a hoarse laugh at his Southport stables with his trainer, Ginger McCain.

Aintree racecourse motor-racing circuit was also once the venue for the world's top drivers, including Fangio and Moss.

Old Liverpool Halls

The great halls and estates of Liverpool's two Earls - Lord Derby and the late Lord Sefton - still stand. This is part of Knowsley Hall, residence of Lord Derby, pictured on 5 June 1949, when it was opened to the public for the first time on a Sunday.

Once the grand residence of the Earls of Sefton, Croxteth Hall and its large estate was opened to the public as a museum and country park, with gardens, lake and animals.

Friends of the Royal Liver Sketching Club visit delightful Speke Hall in June 1931. The hall, on the city side of the Mersey, is Liverpool's most cherished old building. A Tudor, half-timbered hall, it is a Grade 1 listed building and one of the finest examples of its kind in Britain.

17th Century Walton Hall, shortly before its demolition early this century.

Glorious Parks Galore

Sefton Park is one of England's largest parks. Here is the exotic Palm House, damaged in the bombing and now being completely renovated.

Sefton Park's boating lake, as it looked in the early 1930s.

Sunlight and shadows in
lovely Calderstones Park.

Newsham Park's pond in 1955. This has always been a great attraction for young tiddler-fishers - and model boat enthusiasts.

Prince's Park lake and boathouse in the early 1930s.

A sunny stroll in Otterspool Park's 'ravine'.

Admiration for the floral-clock gardeners and their lovely creation in Stanley Park, in 1929.

Birkenhead Park, opened in 1847, was the first major public park. New York's Central Park was created in similar design.

If you go down to the woods today . . .well, in Knowsley Safari Park, anyway, you'll certainly be surprised to find lots of monkey mischief afoot. So, keep those car windows closed!

Liverpool's International Garden Festival

Liverpool took a well-deserved bow in May 1984, when its magnificent International Garden Festival was opened by the Queen to provide a glorious centre, drawing some 3½ million visitors to make it the top tourist attraction. This picture shows part of the 250-acre derelict site being transformed into a floral wonderland in the largest urban land reclamation project undertaken in the U.K.

"What a delightful fragrance" pooch Goldie seems to say, as the Queen, on her Garden Festival tour, meets BBC's Blue Peter presenter, Simon Groom.

The great 'space-age' Festival Hall must have impressed this visiting group, on a Liverpool University course called 'Inside the Garden Festival'.

Some of the gardens were laid out by the countries they represented. This is the Chinese Garden.

The peaceful Indian Garden.

Michael Heseltine, as Minister for Merseyside, admires the Festival Gardens from the bridge of the 'Yellow Submarine', one of the many jolly features.

"Say Cheese!" Going Dutch at the
Festival Lake.

Liverpool-by-the-Sea . . .Part of the fine promenade, built on reclaimed land and partly filled in with rock and earth from
the Queensway Tunnel excavations. It stretches from Garston almost to the city.

Boy Scouts' Jamboree of 1929

The International Boy Scouts' Jamboree, of July 1929, held at Arrowe Park, Birkenhead (the birthplace of the Scout Movement), was opened by the Duke of Connaught and visited by the Prince of Wales and Lord Baden Powell, the Chief Scout. Some 50,000 Scouts, representing 43 nations, in a vast 'tent-town', survived wet and muddy conditions to have the time of their lives.

American Scouts arrive at Liverpool in the liner, Duchess of York, to be greeted by Lord Hampton.

Scout 'braves' perform a
war-dance at the fun-
filled jamboree.

Polish Scouts and Girl Guides
provide a musical turn on the
jamboree field.

The Wonders of Wirral

The beauty spots of Wirral, just 'across the water' from Liverpool, are constantly enjoyed by all Merseysiders. This picture shows the lovely view over the Dee from the heights of Thurstaston Common.

Soap magnate Lord Leverhulme built the model Wirral village of Port Sunlight for his employees in the late Victorian era. Most of the dwellings, in English half-timbered style, with no two groups alike, and with delightful facilities, like the Lady Lever Art Gallery and the Gladstone Theatre, stand within this pretty floral garden estate.

Another Wirral walkway delight: Bidston Hill and its windmill.

Picturesque Parkgate, on the Dee, well known to Nelson's beautiful mistress, Emma, Lady Hamilton, born in the nearby village of Ness.

New Brighton

Shedding clothing at the seaside, like New Brighton here, was simply *infra dig* in the Victorian and Edwardian eras!

But who cares now? . . .Bathing beauties compete for the 1968 'Miss New Brighton' contest.

New Brighton's ferry Pier, now demolished.

A very popular feature of New Brighton was its huge open-air swimming pool, opened by Lord Leverhulme in June 1934, and pictured here at Whitsuntide, 1948.

New Brighton Tower, once Britain's highest structure, but demolished in 1921, rises from 'Little Venice' - part of its surrounding pleasure grounds.

Rough seas attack Fort Perch Rock and the river-mouth lighthouse.

Southport

Sunny Southport (Pleasureland top right) draws crowds of visitors at all seasons.

Lord Street, reckoned to be one of Europe's finest boulevards.

Southport's annual Flower Show is among the best in the world.

Shading trees and ornamental palms lend a 'Continental Air' to this open-air café on Lord Street in August 1933.

"We do like to be beside the seaside" . . .Holidaymakers enjoy sun and music in the Floral Hall gardens.

Royal Birkdale Golf Club's course attracts the world's best golfers. Here are pictured the 1984 organising committee of the Ladies' Scratch Trophy.

And this is how Southport's Pier looked on the occasion of the Duke and Duchess of Teck's visit to the resort in 1872. On the right is the pier's tramway car.

Riverside Recollections

The Port of Liverpool was once 'a forest of masts.' Here is part of it - at George's Dock, where horse-trams crossed a bridge to Mann Island at the Pier Head.

Film star comedian Jimmy 'Schnozzle' Durante lands a 'sole' as he fishes in the Mersey when in Liverpool, appearing at the Empire Theatre, in June 1936. "It's ma foist trip over!" he declared.

'The Bootle Bull', was the nickname for the foghorn on this Gladstone Dock lighthouse, demolished in 1928.

Lowering a cylinder, containing enough gas for a year's supply, into one of the Mersey buoys at Herculaneum Dock.

The Mersey's mighty floating crane, 'Mammoth', at work on New Brighton's landing stage in 1921. She served here for 66 years and her place has now been taken by the new 'Mersey Mammoth'.

Giving vent to religious discussions at the Pier Head's 'Speakers' Corner,' in August 1968.

Tugs galore. These tough little workhorses of the river and docks start up their engines to make a veritable smoke-screen.

Gallant Captain Ian ('Birdseye') North, master of the Liverpool-based Atlantic Conveyor, shortly before sailing into the Falklands War, where his ship was hit by an Argentine missile. About a dozen of the crew died, including Captain North.

The Mersey can show some dangerous teeth in stormy weather!

New Brighton Pier's passenger bridge, damaged by a storm in January 1962.

Boat trips from Liverpool to pretty, wooded Eastham, its hotel and pleasure gardens, were very popular in bygone days, before the ferry was closed.

Mersey entrance to the Ship Canal at Eastham, 36 miles from the Port of Manchester.

The National Waterways
Museum (Boat Museum)
at Ellesmere Port attracts
many visitors.

The old Widnes-Runcorn Transporter, which carried millions of passengers and vehicles high across the Mersey and the
Manchester Ship Canal for 56 years before a new road bridge was opened between the towns in 1961.

Mersey Medley

These little Liverpool waifs typify yesteryear's bare-foot children, many of whom were ill-clothed and under-nourished.

For many years, Christmas came wrapped in a parcel for each of more than 20,000 pre-war poor families and old and infirm people, thanks to the public-sponsored Goodfellow Fund, inaugurated by the *Liverpool Daily Post & Echo* in December 1922. Cooper's, city provision merchants, donated food at cost and hundreds of citizens volunteered their services for packaging and distribution. Pictured: One of the distribution centres in 1935.

Liverpool's May Horse Parade attracted thousands of spectators, especially pre-war. Owners and drivers took the greatest pride in grooming and decorating their charges, drawn chiefly from the Corporation and various businesses.

Teddy Boys (and girls) get carried away in 'Swinging Liverpool' of the 1950s.

Some preferred more sophisticated dancing, like these shown here in the grand finale of the Murphy School Show, at the Grafton Rooms, in May 1959.

Liverpool's fine Georgian and Victorian property constantly attracts film-makers. Here, Percy Street returns to its golden past as a scene from 'The Silk Dress', an S4C drama series, is being produced.

The Liverpool show at Wavertree for many years has proved to be one of the city's prime events. Picture: July 1972.

W.H.J.Jenkins conducts Merseyside Youth Orchestra and Choir at a youth carol service in the Anglican Cathedral.

The Chinese make music in Liverpool, too! This is their community Youth Orchestra.

Prince Charles can hardly forbear to smile as he surveys this vast bread exhibit at the launching of the Tate Gallery of Modern Art at the Albert Dock, in May 1988.

One can see from this very busy Christmas shopping scene in December 1967, why central Church Street was 'pedestrianised'.

It's like shopping in a space-age atmosphere in downtown Liverpool.

Men with a nerve for heights were needed to build St John's Beacon. But what a view from the top!

The old 'wooden-wall' training ship, HMS Conway, anchored in the Mersey for many years, produced many famous sailors. Among her cadets were Poet Laureate John Masefield, Captain Webb, the first person to swim the English Channel, and Lt Ian Fraser VC, of Wallasey. Here, Masefield, fourth from the left, is toasted by Conway cadets on his visit to Liverpool in November 1930.

A bronze Columbus, standing outside Sefton Park's Palm House, views a guard of honour from the US base at Burtonwood, which pays him annual homage on Columbus Day.

1KF -K for Liverpool and F for Ford . . .Liverpool's Lord Mayor (Alderman D.J.Lewis) drives the first Anglia, produced at Ford's Halewood factory, in March 1963.

Right: A resplendent participant in the colourful and musical Caribbean Carnival, which draws thousands of spectators into the city on its annual parade.

Far right: Les Ballets African perform in the new Clayton Square shopping centre, in October 1990.

Liverpool's Chinese Community is the oldest in Europe and has added considerable festivity and colour to the city over many years. Here, in 'Chinatown,' the Lion Dance welcomes the Year of the Tiger.

The first public session of Liverpool's reopened Silver Blades Ice Rink, on 18 March 1960. Liverpool Ice Rink, which produced many champion skaters, including Jeannette Altwegg, holder of the world, European and British titles, opened in September 1931, and closed, for later demolition, on 30 June 1986.

Birkenhead's Hamilton Square - rumoured to be the only 'square-square'!

Subscribers

E Aldersey
Janet B Allan
Dave Allen
Malcolm Stewart Allerton
Paul Allman
Anna Andersen
Mrs G Andrews
Tom Arnison
Helen P Ashton
Mr Stephen Ashton
Fred Askew
Mrs F G Bailey
Florence Ballard
W A Bamford
W G Bamford
J H & B Banahan
William Banks
Mrs Jean Bardgett
Mrs A Barrett
Thomas P Barrett
Mr David A Barrow
B Barry
Mrs B Baxter
Dennis Beacham Sr.
Valerie Beaumont
Irene Beddows
J Berry
J Berry
Jean Billington
Mr Ronald Blackley
P Bland
Mrs S A Blything
George Bordessa
Mr Frank Bourn
Mrs M Boycott
Olive E Bradley
Julie Brett
Mr A T Bright
Alan Briscoe
Henry Brocklehurst
John Bennett Brough
Nicola Bennett Brough
Pamela A Brown
Kenneth E Brunning
J Lewis Burdett
George William Burgess
William Burridge
William Butters
David Cain
Peter Gregory Callan
Mrs Susan Carrick
Maureen Carroll
Joanne Carson
Alan S Carter
Joan Cartwright (née Moore)
Wesley James Cave
W H Chalton

J Cherry
Terence Claeys
David Clark
Alan Clarke
Joseph Claus
Mrs Florence Clougher
Neale Coleman
Charles Collier
James Collier
Leslie James Collin
Peter Connell
Philip Connell
John Cooke
Peter Cooke
Peter James Cooper
Henry F Copland
Copeland, Gladys & Bob
E P Corkhill
J C Cosgrove
W R Courtliffe
Joyce Coventry
K W Crick
Leslie Crierie
Laura Crisp
Ronnie Cunningham
Con Currie
Jacqueline Currie
Mrs Linda Dagnall
Alan Malcolm Dale
Geoff Dalzell
Sue Dalzell
H W Danson, for Golden Wedding
James Davies
Mrs Margaret Davies
Ron Dawson
Dr Alan J Day
George Dean
J A Delaney
Mr A Deveney
Robina S Dexter
J & K Donnelly
W L M Douglas
Tom & Nancy Dowd
Mr J Downey
John W Doyle
Mrs Doris Durband
James Dykes
G Eccles
Mr Stephen Edwards
William E Ellis
Francis John Entwistle
Brian Evans, F.R.I.B.A.
Mr Eric Evans
Ellen Fariss
Mr David Farmer
David Findlay
R Finegan

Joseph Fitzsimmons
Albert Fletcher
Barbara Forshaw
Barbara Forshaw
Chris Forshaw
Douglas Forsyth
Hilda J Foster
Robert Anthony Fox
Joe Franckel
Mr Ronald Francom
Roy Franks
John French
Leslie French
Arthur Frith
Robert J Frith
Anthony Gallagher
Lilian Gamble
Ronald W Garland
Anne Georgeson
Hilda Getty
E Gibson
Kay Gilchrist
Eddie Gillbanks
Norman Gilligan
Joe Glover
V Glover
Mrs M Goldstraw
Graham Goodwin
James Goss
Jean Grant
Mrs L Greatbatch
Mrs Edna Mary Griffiths
James W Griffiths
John Gudgeon
Alexander Guy
Lawrence Haigh
Beatrice Mary Hallam, on her 80th birthday
William Hallaron
Elizabeth Hambleton
Michael Handley
Robert Hanratty
Mr Thomas Hanson
Michael G Harris
R Henderson
Shirley Henney
Adrian Herbaut
Derek Hewitt
Marion Heywood
James E Hibbins
M P Higgins
A I Highet
L D Hignett
Ted Hillman
Michael Hinde
Stanley Hinde
James Hitchen
E A Hogben
L Holden
Frank James Holland

Bert Hornby
Miss N Hornby
Alex C Hughes
G R Hughes
Mrs Mary Hughes
Sarah Hughes
Stephen Paul Hughes
Richard A Hunt
Miss L J M Husband
Bette & Colin Hutchison
Ann & Brian Jackson
Miss C C Jansson
R H Johnson
T N Johnston
Esther Joinson (California, USA)
Andrew W Jones
G B Jones
Les Jones
R O Jones
Barry Jordon
J Charles Jump
George Alexander Kean
W Keane
Hannah Keegan
Malcolm C Keenan
Mrs B J Keig
Mr J Kelly
John F Kelly
Kenneth R Kelly
Mr W Kelly
Vivienne Rive Kennils
Kenneth King
Robert King
Mrs F Kneale
Mrs V Lawrence
June Lebroc
Mrs A M Leighton
John Lennon
Brian Leonard
Mr Len Leonard
J Leyland
John Geoffrey Lindley
Lindsey Helen Ling
A J & N C Little
Jane Livesey
Maisie Livesey
E Lowe
T H Lowe
George Lucas
William Lucas
Elsie (Lord) Luongo
Arthur P McArdle
Mr R McBride
Sheila M McCann
N F McClemens
Martin J McDonough
E McDougall (Sarasota, USA)
Ron MacFall
Paul McGaw

Mrs McGee
Kathleen M McKee
Ronald McLeod
Joseph McMahon
D McMath
George McNabb
Mr Edward McNamara
Patricia McShane
Paul McTigue
James Malone
Robbie Marshall
Robert H Meade
Mr Michael Melling
Eric James Melvin
Mrs L M Miller
Mrs P Mills
Pauline Mills
Bob & Ethel Mitchell
Harry Mitchell
John & Brian Mitchell
Phil Mobbs
Dennis James Moffatt
Joan A Mooney
John Mooney
S J Moorcroft
Mr Brian Moore
Eric Edward Moore
Claire Moorhead
Phil Morley
Mrs Alice Elizabeth Moulton
Ian J Mowat
David & Elizabeth Murphy
Elizabeth Murphy
Francis M Murphy
Geoffrey P Naylor
Michael Robert Newport
C G Newton
E R Newton
Bobby Nick (Accordionist)
D V G Nicholson
Mr Alan Orbison
Mr Joseph O'Shaughnessy
David J Owens
Hilary Oxlade
Thomas Park
John Parker
Mr L Parry
Mrs D Parry
Mrs Sheila Paterson
Winifred Pearce
Debra Pearlman
John Pearlman
Paul Perry
Mrs Audrey Peters
D H Petherbridge
Brian R Phillips
Mr Frank Phillips
George Phippard
Albert E Pollard

Richard Powell
John Price
Mrs R Proudfoot
Anthony Putt
William Quayle
Gordon E Quigley
Edward Radcliffe
Paul N Radcliffe
Gordon Radley
Mr Donald Redmond
William Reid
Elizabeth Rhodes
James Richards
Mr L G Richmond
Mary Riley
Francis Rimmer
Mrs Sarah Rizzotti
Alan, Julie, Kenny Roberts
Marjorie Roberts
P G Roberts B.A., B.Arch.
Roy Roberts
Mrs Sandria Catherine Roberts
Stanley Roberts
Steve 'Scouse' Roberts
W T Roberts
Peter A Rogan
Teresa Rogers
Leslie A Rolls
P E Rooney
Ronald Lyle Rowson
Robert A Rudkin
Richard Rummens
Gerard Sainsbury
Mrs J C Salt
Francis Sanders
J J Sanders
Antony Sartorius
John Saville
Gerard Schaer
Alex Schouler
Enid Schwerin
Thomas Sefton
Vera A Shallcross
Mrs P A Shepherd
R & J Shepherd
Frank Short
Edward Sixsmith
Robert Skillicorn
S Slavin
Derek C Smith
James A Smith
F M Southcote
Mr Stanley A Stafford
Mr & Mrs F J Startup
J Barrie R Steadman
W Lawrence Steadman
Tracey Steele
Maroulla Stephanides
Carol Storey

M D Stott
Roger Stowe
Mrs A L Sutton
Joyce Swallow
Charles & Clare Swift
Mr James Peter Taker
David Taylor
George Taylor
Sqn Ldr J C Taylor
K Taylor
W G Taylor
Mr Joseph Thistlewaite
J E Thomas
J H Tinosley
Alan Toft
Patricia Tyrer
C J Usher
John A Vaughan
Paula Vance (USA)
Graham Walker
Malcolm Walker
Margaret Walker
Nora Ellen Walker
Mrs T Walker (Australia)
F T Wallace
Harold Walsh

Caroline Louise Ward
Mr David Weaver
William Webster
E Weeden
Frank & Joan Welsh
G Wharton
S Wharton
S Wharton
Mrs K Whearty
Kate Whitehead
Kathleen Whitehead
Maureen Whitehead
Ted Whitehead
Malcolm John Whittle
Kevin Wilde
Mrs M Wilkins
Pat Wilkinson
Mr Frank Williams
J Williams
Mrs Nora Williams
George Winstanley
Mrs Leta Youings
Mrs Ethel (Pearl) Young
James Young
Rosemary Young